DARTMOOR

A new look at the views that illustrated
Crossing's Guide to Dartmoor,
researched and introduced by the
illustrator's grandson,
Andrew Stevens

Peninsula
Press

Front Cover: THE WINDYPOST - (looking ENE) (OS 534743) This rather dark drawing, suggesting evening shadows, is similar to that on page 148 of *Crossing's Guide to Dartmoor*, but it is unique in being the only drawing to have survived, and it has never been published before.

Crossing's Guide to Dartmoor is published by Peninsula Press.
For a complete stock list of Peninsula Press titles, please send an s.a.e. to the address below.

Published by Peninsula Press Ltd
P.O. Box 31
Newton Abbot
Devon TQ12 5XH
Tel: 0803 875875

© Andrew Stevens 1994

Printed in England by
R.Booth Ltd, Penryn, Cornwall.

ISBN 1 872640 14 1

CONTENTS

Princetown & Two Bridges Distrct

From Double Waters looking S.W. 7

Burrator Lake from Cramber Tor 7

Peat Cot from S.Hisworthy Tor 8

From Main Road near New London 8

From above Wistman's Wood 9

From road about 100 yards S. of Rundlestone 9

Looking N.N.E. from Mis Tor 10

Looking N.E. from Mis Tor 10

From Ashburton road beyond Two Bridges 11

From Ashburton road beyond Two Bridges 11

Tavistock District

From Windy Post looking N.E. 12

From Barn Hill 1/4 mile N. of Windy Post 12

From Gibbet Hill (N.E. by N.) 13

From Gibbet Hill 13

From Gibbet Hill 14

From Gibbet Hill 14

From Gibbet Hill (S.E. by S.) 15

Lydford District

From Watern Oke looking E. 15

Okehampton District

From Moor Brook looking S. 16

From High Willes 16

From High Willes 17

Chagford & Moreton District

From Walla Brook Clapper looking W. 17

From near Warren House Inn looking E. 18

Bovey Tracey District

From Holwell Down looking E. 18

From Holwell Down looking S. 19

From half-way up Widecombe Hill looking N. 19

Ashburton District

From Bel Tor looking W. 20

Brent & Ivybridge District

From Holne road, W. of reservoir, looking N.N.E. 20

From Holne road W. of reservoir 21

From Combestone Tor looking N. 21

From Hickaton Hill, Dean Moor, looking S.W. 22

From Petres Cross looking N.W. 22

From Green Hill looking S.S.E. 23
From Butterdon Hill looking N.E. 23
From Butterdon Hill looking N. 24
From Tristis Rock looking N. 24
From Southern Slope of Stalldon Barrow looking S.E. 25
From Broad Rock looking S.E. 25
From near Broad Rock looking N.W. 26
From near Broad Rock 26

Plympton & Shaugh District
From Whitehall Corner looking E. 27
From Blackaton Cross looking N. 27
From near Cadaford Bridge 28
From Cadaford Bridge 28

Yelverton District
From near Roborough Rock 29
From near Roborough Rock 29
From near Roborough Rock 30
From summit of Peak Hill looking N.E. 30
From summit of Peak Hill 31
From pond on Peak Hill looking N. 31
From pond on Peak Hill 32

Hexworthy District
From Forest Inn, Hexworthy 32
From road at top of Dartmeet Hill looking due S. 33
From road near Huccaby Cottage 33
From Swincombe Newtake looking N. by E. 34

Postbridge District
From Lakehead Hill looking N.E. 34
From Soussons Common looking W. 35
From Soussons Common looking N.E. 35
From Meripit Hill looking S.W. 36
From road at Lakehead Hill looking W. to N.W. 36
From near Archerton looking N.N.E. 37
From Cut Hill looking N. 37
From 1/4 mile W. of E. Dart Head 38
From Little Kneeset looking N.E. 38
From S. slope of Okement Hill 1/4 mile S.E. of summit 39
From near summit of Newtake 39
From Newtake 1/3 mile S. of summit 40
From near E. Dart Head 40

INTRODUCTION

Many books have been written about Dartmoor and a few have become almost legendary. All aspects have been well documented, yet only one person has attempted to write a comprehensive and integrated description of the whole area with the rambler in mind. He was William Crossing and his book is *Crossing's Guide to Dartmoor*. Prior to this, access to the moor for the traveller had been rather limited. Increasingly the best approach had been by railway: Yelverton and Tavistock by 1859; Lydford by 1865; Moretonhampstead by 1866; Okehampton by 1871; Ashburton by 1872 and finally the remarkable branch from Yelverton to Princetown via Dousland and Burrator in 1883. By the turn of the century the number of visitors had increased enormously, but nothing compared to what was to come as a result of the next transport revolution in the form of the charabanc and private motor car.

Some guidance for the visitor was becoming a necessity and Crossing set out to produce something that was more than just a series of physical references, background information, social, historical and anecdotal, enriched the text throughout. At some point during his research for the book, he realised the need for some visual content and sought the services of an illustrator, but it would have to be someone local with a love for, and intimate knowledge of, the moor. Philip Guy Stevens had been brought up in Princetown and attended Tavistock Grammer School, often walking the seven miles to school rather than taking the train via Yelverton. Much of his spare time had been spent walking and camping on the moor and latterly he had begun painting in oils and watercolours. P.G.S. (as everyone knew him) accepted Crossing's commission, but it was agreed that the illustrations were to be in pen and ink, partly, no doubt for ease of printing, but also because this would be the best medium for portraying hills and tors in silhouette against the skyline.

The drawings were produced quickly. Crossing would leave instructions by telegraph and, to comply, P.G.S. would walk to the appropriate location, make the sketch and return, often before going to work. In the published reproductions of the sketches, many show marks in the corners where the originals had been pinned. These circular marks, either white on black or black on white must not be confused with the actual content of the sketches! Sixty-eight sketches were reproduced in Crossing's book but only one of these originals appears to have survived (see page 2).

Crossing's Guide to Dartmoor, complete with sketches, was first published in 1909, and most recently in 1990 by Peninsula Press. In 1983 P.G.S.'s son Alan and daughter Barbara republished the sketches, without any text or map references. This book is therefore an attempt to produce a compromise, somewhere between the original context of the sketches and this recent context-less publication. Here, each of the original sketches is presented with a page reference from the original *Guide,* a four or six-figure map reference, and some brief information about the location, showing the visible changes after nearly a century.

Since the first publication of *Crossing's Guide,* Dartmoor itself, as a natural environment, has not really changed at all. Nevertheless, the modern visitor will witness a variety of visible changes, with reference to the sketches. These visible differences are all man-made or man-induced, such as afforestation. Tree management really began on Dartmoor during the early 19th century. There were various schemes to rehabilitate derelict woodlands or to establish new plantations. Another factor for change was water management. Water has always been managed by humans as a resource, and on Dartmoor large storage reservoirs were established. Necessary or not, aesthetically pleasing or not, reservoirs fundamentally transform the visual aspects of an area both in terms of the valleys and features they obscure and the new environments they create.

The scene when Crossing wrote his *Guide* was very different to the present one, with respect to mining. The tin mines and granite quarries (except at Merrivale) are all closed, and china clay has been the growth industry, and continues to have considerable visual impact on the moor.

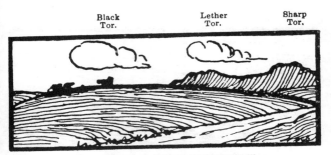

Black
Tor.

Lether
Tor.

Sharp
Tor.

FROM DOUBLE WATERS, LOOKING S.W.

CROSSING page reference: 90 O.S.MAP reference: SX 575725
TITLE: FROM DOUBLE WATERS LOOKING S.W.
Double Waters is not named on the map, but it is the next significant causeway after Devil's Bridge on the B3212 Princetown to Yelverton road. Black Tor has a logan stone within its rock formation, but not one that pivots easily. The view is virtually unchanged today, apart from the appearance of the road, shown as the track in the foreground. Sharp Tor now appears as Sharpitor and Lether Tor is now Leather Tor.

Lether Tor

BURRATOR LAKE FROM CRAMBER TOR.

CROSSING page reference: 98 O.S.MAP reference: SX 583712
TITLE: BURRATOR LAKE FROM CRAMBER TOR
Burrator Lake was the first water authority reservoir on Dartmoor, constructed to satisfy the growing demands of the expanding city of Plymouth, and fed by two tributary streams, the Newleycombe Lake and the Narrator Brook, coming in on the left between Cramber Tor and Sheeps Tor. The granite dam across the River Meavy (Mewey) was raised in 1928, about 20 years after the sketch was drawn. The scene today has been radically altered by the growth of conifers planted in 1937, which almost surround the lake.

Ter Hill.   Stream Hill.   Hand Hill.

PEAT COT FROM SOUTH HISWORTHY TOR.

CROSSING page reference: 103 O.S.MAP reference: SX597723
TITLE: PEAT COT FROM SOUTH HISWORTHY TOR
Hisworthy is now Hessary, but the tor with its iron spike pointing skywards from the summit and the view from it looking south eastwards have changed little, apart from one of the Peat Cot dwellings being obscured by trees. The Devonport leat can be seen on the left following the contours as it carries its precious load towards Burrator Reservoir.

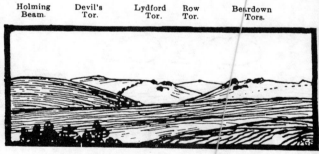

Holming Beam.   Devil's Tor.   Lydford Tor.   Row Tor.   Beardown Tors.

FROM MAIN ROAD NEAR NEW LONDON.

CROSSING page reference: 111 O.S.MAP reference: SX 592786
TITLE: FROM MAIN ROAD NEAR NEW LONDON
The main road is the B3212 which leaves Princetown Square for Two Bridges. New London is the housing development on the right. The last house on the left has been extended where previously there had been a courtyard, from which this sketch was probably made. The view faces roughly north-east with the main road on the right and the prison on the left. The only significant difference is that the top and left-hand side of Holming Beam is now afforested (Long Plantation).

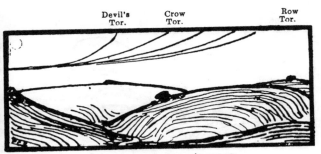

Devil's Tor.   Crow Tor.   Row Tor.

FROM ABOVE WISTMAN'S WOOD.

CROSSING page reference:116 O.S.MAP reference: SX 6177
TITLE: FROM ABOVE WISTMAN'S WOOD
Wistman's Wood is most easily approached up the West Dart Valley
from Two Bridges. It is one of only three ancient oak woods on the
open moor, and best known because of its folklore. It is a mysterious,
atmospheric place with twisted trunks emerging from the granite
clitter which is carpeted with bright green moss. Neither the wood
nor the view have changed significantly this century. Just the
northern end of the extensive Bairdown (now Beardown) Tors is
depicted. Row Tor on the right is now spelt Rough.

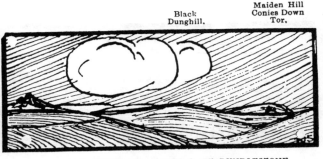

Black Dunghill.   Maiden Hill Conies Down Tor.   Holming Beam.

FROM ROAD ABOUT 100 YARDS S. OF RUNDLESTONE.

CROSSING page reference: 123 O.S.MAP reference: SX 577748
TITLE: FROM ROAD ABOUT 100 YARDS S. OF
RUNDLESTONE
This view is looking roughly north, but the sketch uses considerable
artistic licence. The white high ground to the right of Mis Tor is
Cocks Hill. The line contouring the near hill below Mis Tor is the
prison leat, although now the open water course ends in a little
holding reservoir in an enclosure to the north of the main Two
Bridges/Tavistock road at its junction with the Princetown road
(from where this sketch must have been drawn).

Gt. Links Tor.   Waternoke Lynch Tor.   High Willes.

LOOKING N.N.E. FROM MIS TOR.

CROSSING page reference: 124 O.S.MAP reference: SX 562770
TITLE: LOOKING N.N.E. FROM MIS TOR

Great Mis Tor is an impressive and outstanding landmark from most directions. It is most easily approached from the main road at Rundlestone where a track leads out through the settlement enclosures to the open moor. It is just over eight miles 'as the crow flies' from Mis Tor to High Willes (now Willhays), and the sketch has left out some of the intermediary detail. Waternoke (written as two words now) is the area north of the River Tavy, below its junction with the Amicombe Brook at Sandy Ford.

Gt. Kneeset.   Walkham Hd.   Fur Tor.   Cut Hill.

Slope of High Willes.

LOOKING N.E. FROM MIS TOR.

CROSSING page reference: 125 O.S.MAP reference: SX 562770
TITLE: LOOKING N.E. FROM MIS TOR

The view shown in the sketch has not visibly changed at all. The near valley is that of the River Walkham which turns sharply left and runs up behind the nearest high ground (Cocks Hill), not named on this sketch. The distance from Mis Tor to Fur Tor is only just over four miles in a straight line - but a direct route is not practical because of the terrain between the two points.

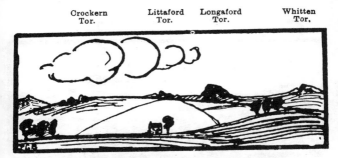

Crockern Tor.   Littaford Tor.   Longaford Tor.   Whitten Tor.

FROM ASHBURTON ROAD BEYOND TWO BRIDGES.
NEAR PRINCEHALL LODGE.

CROSSING page reference: 131 O.S.MAP reference: SX 621747
TITLE: FROM ASHBURTON ROAD BEYOND TWO BRIDGES, NEAR PRINCEHALL LODGE

The building in the central foreground is now part of Spaders Farm. The hill behind now supports considerable tree growth and this currently obscures Littaford and Longaford Tors beyond. The group of trees on the left of the sketch shows the location of Parson's Cottage, which was in ruins at that time. Whitten Tor was also referred to by Crossing using its modern name Higher White Tor.

Bellaford Tor.   Hameldon.   Lough Tor.

FROM ASHBURTON ROAD BEYOND TWO BRIDGES.
NEAR PRINCEHALL LODGE.

CROSSING page reference: 131 O.S.MAP reference: SX 624746
TITLE: FROM ASHBURTON ROAD BEYOND TWO BRIDGES, NEAR PRINCEHALL LODGE

Prince Hall had been one of Dartmoor's Ancient Tenements and is currently a hotel. The view from here is considerably different now due to the extensive conifer plantations which now surround Bellaford and Lough Tors (now Bellever and Laughter Tors). The far ridge of Hameldon (now Hamel Down) can still just be seen above the tree line. The valley in the foreground carries the Muddilake Brook which joins the Cherry Brook just above Lower Cherrybrook Bridge (SX 631748).

Cocks Tor. Staple Tors.

Barn Hill.

FROM WINDY POST, LOOKING N.E.

CROSSING page reference: 148 O.S.MAP reference: SX 533741
TITLE: FROM WINDY POST, LOOKING N.E.
Windy Post is the common name for the granite cross shown in the
near foreground, dating back to the sixteenth century and which
marks an ancient pathway across the moor, linking Chagford with
Tavistock. The two lines on the right of the cross were leats. The
upper one is now dry, but the lower one, called Grimstone Leat, is
still used and divides just beyond the cross. The two parts of Staple
Tor are now separately named as Middle and Great Staple Tors.

Cocks Tor. Staple Tors.

FROM BARN HILL, ¼ M. NORTH OF WINDY POST.

CROSSING page reference: 148 O.S.MAP reference: SX 534746
TITLE: FROM BARN HILL, 1/4 M. NORTH OF WINDY POST
The horizontal line of poles in the middle foreground marks the
road from Princetown to Tavistock, now the B3357. These would
have carried the telegraph lines which have long since been removed.
The two distinct parts of Staple Tor are clearly shown. Cocks Tor is
particularly impressive when approached from the west, since it is
the first major feature to be seen after climbing Pork Hill out of
Tavistock.

Sourton. Corn Great Links Dunnagoat Sharp
Tors. Ridge. Tor. Tors. Tor.

Noddon. Arms Bra Doe
N.E. by N. Tor. Tor. Tor.

FROM GIBBET HILL.

CROSSING page reference: 158 O.S.MAP reference: SX 503811
TITLE: FROM GIBBET HILL
P.G.S. has taken some artistic licence in this drawing, bringing the features closer. The foreground is a broad expanse of uncultivated grassland. Bra Tor was originally Brattor and the current compromise is Brat Tor! The steep sided valley of the River Lyd, from which Noddon (now Great Nodden) rises, marks the western edge of the granite rock. Nodden itself is largely composed of altered slate.

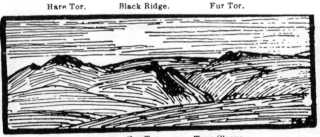

Hare Tor. Black Ridge. Fur Tor.

Ger Tor. Tavy Cleave.
FROM GIBBET HILL.

CROSSING page reference: 158 O.S.MAP reference: SX 503811
TITLE: FROM GIBBET HILL
If you were to place the left hand edge of this sketch alongside the right hand edge of the other sketch on this page of *Crossing's Guide*, you would see that the one is a continuation of the other. Ger Tor is the nearest named feature and stands as a sentinel overlooking the entrance to Tavy Cleave. Fur Tor and Black Ridge are twice as far away on the most remote area of the northern moor.

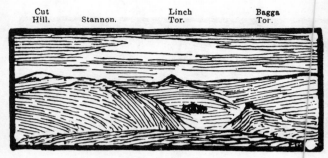

Cut Hill.   Stannon.   Linch Tor.   Bagga Tor.

FROM GIBBET HILL.

CROSSING page reference: 159 O.S.MAP reference: SX 503811
TITLE: FROM GIBBET HILL
This sketch continues the panoramic view from Gibbet Hill, working from north to south, and therefore it can be placed alongside the second sketch on page 158 of *Crossing's Guide*. Cut Hill is in the far distance with Fur Tor on its near left. The dark area on the steep slopes of Linch Tor (now Lynch), represents the trees of South Common Plantation. Bagga Tor is not as prominent and separate as depicted in the sketch.

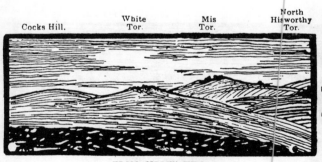

Cocks Hill.   White Tor.   Mis Tor.   North Hisworthy Tor.   Roose Tor.

FROM GIBBET HILL.

CROSSING page reference: 159 O.S.MAP reference: SX 503811
TITLE: FROM GIBBET HILL
"The chief interest of Gibbet Hill is the wonderful picture seen from its summit." (*Crossing's Guide*, page 159.) This is the fourth in the series of five sketches depicting the panorama to the east. The skyline is featured to the exclusion of any foreground detail, which is a pity, as the broad valley of the River Tavy below presents a beautiful contrast to the rough moorland beyond.

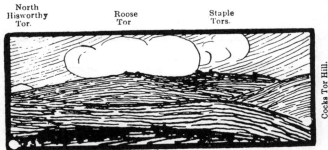

North Hisworthy Tor

Roose Tor

Staple Tors.

Cocks Tor Hill.

S.E. by S.

FROM GIBBET HILL.

CROSSING page reference: 160 O. S. MAP reference: SX 503811
TITLE: FROM GIBBET HILL
"The hill obtains its name from the hideous object said once to
have been erected here. The road over the down...had the evil
reputation of being infested with highwaymen, and this hill being
in view from it...was deemed a fitting place on which to expose the
bodies of malefactors who had suffered at the hands of the law."
(*Crossing's Guide*, page 158). North Hisworthy Tor is less obvious
than the drawing suggests, but with clear visibility, it can be easily
identified now by the communications mast on its summit.

Black Hill.

Fur Tor.

Amicombe Bend.

The Meads.

The Tavy.

FROM WATERN OKE, LOOKING E.

CROSSING page reference: 175 O. S. MAP reference: SX 566834
TITLE: FROM WATERN OKE, LOOKING E.
The spot from which this drawing was made must have been close
to the Bronze Age Settlement which is located on this north bank
of the River Tavy. The sketch does not attempt to show that this
river bends sharply right around the Meads and is joined at Sandy
Ford by the Amicombe Brook coming in from the left. The walk up
Tavy Cleave to this location from Lane End (SX 537823) is
reputedly one of the most dramatic on Dartmoor.

Row Tor.   West Mill Tor.   Yes Tor.

FROM MOOR BROOK, LOOKING S.

CROSSING page reference: 199 O.S.MAP reference: SX 591930
TITLE: FROM MOOR BROOK, LOOKING S.
The Moor Brook itself is rather more defined than indicated in the sketch and has a rough military track alongside it on the right. Row Tor is a little less angular than the drawing suggests and set a little more to the left. The flag pole clearly indicated in the sketch is out of all proportion and is probably shown only because Crossing specifically mentions it in his text.

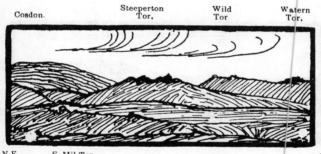

Cosdon.   Steeperton Tor.   Wild Tor   Watern Tor.

E N E.   E. Mil Tor.   S.E.

FROM HIGH WILLES.

CROSSING page reference: 202 O.S.MAP reference: SX 581894
TITLE: FROM HIGH WILLES
The sketch could never hope to have captured just how impressive this view can be, and how different it can look on each visit. Wherever you stand, it seems impossible to line up all the features as depicted in this sketch! Moreover, Metheral Hill, which is clearly visible between Cosdon and Steeperton Tor is completely missing! Perhaps P.G.S. left it out deliberately just because it is featureless?

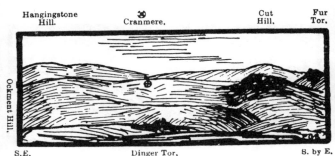

FROM HIGH WILLES.

CROSSING page reference: 203 O.S.MAP reference: SX 580891
TITLE: FROM HIGH WILLES
The view from here is both panoramic and spectacular. Great
Kneeset, below Cut Hill, is shown as if it were as rocky as Fur Tor,
but it is not. Perhaps the shading was to indicate the blackness of
the peat which covers the whole area. The high point to the right of
Hangingstone Hill is Whitehorse Hill. These days, Hangingstone
Hill is distinctive because of the army observation post on top.

FROM WALLA BROOK CLAPPER, LOOKING WEST.

CROSSING page reference: 257 O.S.MAP reference: SX 653871
TITLE: FROM WALLA BROOK CLAPPER, LOOKING W.
Apart from the more recent growth of a small, lonely hawthorn tree
by the bridge itself, the view to the west remains unchanged. The
ridge to the left of Wild Tor is in fact higher than the tor itself, yet
the sketch does not give this impression. The wall on the left marks
the furthest boundary of what was Teignhead Farm, now abandoned
and in ruins.

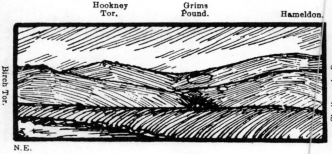

Hookney Tor. Grims Pound. Hameldon.

Birch Tor. Challacombe Down.

N.E.

FROM NEAR WARREN HOUSE INN, LOOKING E.

CROSSING page reference: 261 O.S.MAP reference: SX 673806
TITLE: FROM NEAR WARREN HOUSE INN, LOOKING E.
The telephone line to Headland Warren is a more recent addition to the scene. The sketch omits the ancient pound on the slopes of Birch Tor. The obvious track in that location is more recent. The central dark area on the middle horizon (below Grimspound) is the nearest the sketch comes to depicting the scars left by earlier mining activities. The tips of the conifer trees emerging from the W.Webbern valley beyond Challacombe are part of the more recent Soussons plantation.

Hey Tor. Saddle Tor.

Leighon Tor.

Smallacombe Rocks. Holwell Tor.

FROM HOLWELL DOWN, LOOKING E.

CROSSING page reference: 312 O.S.MAP reference: SX 737766
TITLE: FROM HOLWELL DOWN, LOOKING E.
This location is best approached on the country road from Bovey Tracey to Widecombe. If you stop at Harefoot Cross and take up position on the slopes above the road, the view to the north-east is very similar to this sketch, except that Emsworthy Rocks should be in line with Haytor Rocks, with Holwell Tor and Smallacombe Rocks on the left. In any event the view is quite spectacular!

Rippon Tor.   The Nutcracker.

FROM HOLWELL DOWN, LOOKING S.

CROSSING page reference: 313 O.S.MAP reference: SX 7376
TITLE: FROM HOLWELL DOWN, LOOKING S.
Although Rippon Tor is roughly south of Holwell Down, the sketch
was probably not made from that location, but more likely from the
slopes of Top Tor, above Harefoot Cross. The foreground suggests
this, as does the alignment of the wall which disappears over the
left shoulder of Rippon Tor. The Nutcracker was well known for its
logan stone, but unfortunately this was vandalised in the 1970s,
and is no longer marked by name on recent O.S. maps.

                           Chinkwell   Bel   Bonehill
Hameldon.   Tor.   Tor.   Rocks.

FROM HALF-WAY UP WIDECOMBE HILL, LOOKING N.

CROSSING page reference: 314 O. S. MAP reference: SX 726767
TITLE: FROM HALF-WAY UP WIDECOMBE HILL, LOOKING
N.
Widecombe Hill is famous, along with Tom Pearse's old grey mare,
in the song about Widecombe Fair. The dry stone wall in the right
foreground is on the far side of the road. The view has changed
little, apart from the increased vegetation and the red-tiled house
which has been built since. Bel Tor now appears as Bell Tor.

Combestone Tor.   Sharp Tor.

Holne Moor.

FROM BEL TOR, LOOKING W.

CROSSING page reference: 337 O.S.MAP reference: SX 6973
TITLE: FROM BEL TOR, LOOKING W.
Judging by the absence of foreground detail, this drawing was
probably done from the track to the west of the walled enclosure.
This drawing is interesting in that it is the only one which clearly
indicates the time of day (i.e. sunset) and, in view of the position of
the sun itself, two possible times of year - either early spring or late
autumn. The high ground behind Combestone Tor is Down Ridge.

Yar   Corndon   Sharp   Chinkwell   Bel   Mil
Tor.   Tor.   Tor.   Hameldon.   Tor.   Tor. Tor.

Road to Rowbrook.

FROM HOLNE ROAD, W. OF RESERVOIR, LOOKING N.N.E.

CROSSING page reference: 359 O.S.MAP reference: SX 6871
TITLE: FROM HOLNE ROAD, W. OF RESERVOIR, LOOKING
N.N.E.
This sketch was probably drawn from a standpoint near to where
the original course of the Holne Moor leat is interrupted. Between
this point where the leat disappears, and Sharp Tor, is the Double
Dart gorge with the track to Rowbrook, now metalled, leading down
into it. Mil Tor is now Mel Tor. Bel Tor in this location should not
be confused with Bell Tor which is below distant Chinkwell Tor
and therefore hidden by the nearer horizon!

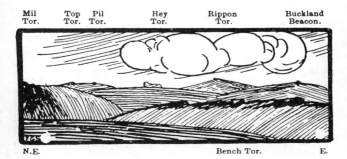

| Mil Tor. | Top Tor. | Pil Tor. | Hey Tor. | Rippon Tor. | Buckland Beacon. |

N.E.   Bench Tor.   E.

FROM HOLNE ROAD, W. OF RESERVOIR.

CROSSING page reference: 360 O.S.MAP reference: SX 683713
TITLE: FROM HOLNE ROAD, W. OF RESERVOIR
The vantage point for this sketch must have been up the hill at a
point about 75yards beyond where the Holne Moor Leat disappears
down a pipe by the roadside. The long ridge of Bench Tor dominates
the near horizon. On the right there is now a prominent group of
trees on the far horizon between Rippon Tor and Buckland Beacon.
Distant Hay Tor can be seen, but over the top of what must be
Saddle Tor.

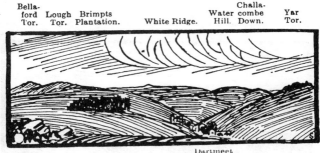

| Bellaford Tor. | Lough Tor. | Brimpts Plantation. | White Ridge. | Water Hill. | Challacombe Down. | Yar Tor. |

Dartmeet Bridge.

FROM COMBESTONE TOR, LOOKING N.

CROSSING page reference: 361 O.S.MAP reference: SX 670718
TITLE: FROM COMBESTONE TOR, LOOKING N.
Combestone Tor is satirically known as 'the tourist's tor', because
of its proximity to the country road which links Hexworthy with
Holne. The view from this tor overlooks another of the tourist 'hot
spots'- Dartmeet. Nevertheless, this is a beautiful spot overlooking
the double Dart gorge. If you wish to walk to the facilities at
Dartmeet, then be warned - you can cross the West Dart only over
stepping stones and then only at low tide!

Eastern Whitaburrow.   Western Whitaburrow.   Huntingdon Warren.

FROM HICKATON HILL, DEAN MOOR, LOOKING S.W.

CROSSING page reference: 366 O.S.MAP reference: SX 670667
TITLE: FROM HICKATON HILL, DEAN MOOR, LOOKING S.W.

There is a well marked, grassy track from the lane at Lud Gate (SX 684673) straight up over the shoulder of Pupers Hill, and on to the ford below Huntingdon Warren. The sketch is accurate but represents a very wide angle of view - about 100 degrees. No buildings have survived at Huntingdon Warren, only the surrounding enclosures. East and West Whitabarrow (now E. and W. White Barrow) are beyond the River Avon, which is now dammed further downstream.

Staple Roose N. His- Mis Gt. Links Maiden Bairdow
Tor. Tor. worthy Tor. Tor. Tor. Hill. Tor.

Erne Valley.   Avon Valley.

FROM PETRES CROSS. LOOKING N.W.

CROSSING page reference: 371 O. S. MAP reference: SX 653654
TITLE: FROM PETRE'S CROSS, LOOKING N.W.

Petre's Cross is no longer a cross. Around 1847, the granite upright was used for a roof support in the now ruined stone house that was erected on the top of Western White Barrow as sheltered accommodation. Prominent in the foreground now is the conical spoil tip of the Red Lake China Clay works. N. Hisworthy Tor, the nearest named feature, is eight miles away - whereas Great Links Tor is approximately fifteen miles distant and therefore less often actually visible.

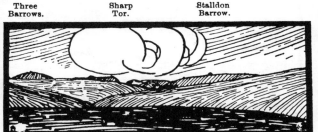

Three Barrows. Sharp Tor. Stalldon Barrow.

Brown Heath.

Outer Stall Moor.

FROM GREEN HILL. LOOKING S.S.E.

CROSSING page reference: 373 O.S.MAP reference: SX 636677
TITLE: FROM GREEN HILL, LOOKING S.S.E.
Green Hill was probably so called because it was considered to provide some of the best pasturage on the moor. A track passes Green Hill on the left and on the right, almost due east of Green Hill, above Blacklane Brook, is Duck's Pool. Here, in addition to the letter-box, is the memorial plaque to William Crossing, which reads:-
IN MEMORY OF WILLIAM CROSSING, AUTHOR OF MANY INSPIRING BOOKS ON DARTMOOR, WHOSE GUIDE IS A SOURCE OF INVALUABLE INFORMATION TO ALL LOVERS OF THE MOOR. DIED 3RD SEP 1928 AGED 80

Cairns. Ugborough Beacon.

Cairns.

FROM BUTTERDON HILL. LOOKING N.E.

CROSSING page reference: 394 O.S.MAP reference: SX 655586
TITLE: FROM BUTTERDON HILL, LOOKING N.E.
There are three cairns on Butterdon Hill and it would appear that this sketch was drawn from the one on the summit. There are at least three distinct folds of land on the moor itself beyond the cairn to the left, including the high features of Dean Moor and Brent Moor. To the south of this location is Western Beacon which is the most southerly prominence on Dartmoor.

Stalldon
Barrow.

Sharp
Tor.

Three
Barrows.

Eastern
Whitaburrow.

Piles Hill. Hangershell
Rock.

FROM BUTTERDON HILL. LOOKING N.

CROSSING page reference: 395 O.S.MAP reference: SX 655586
TITLE: FROM BUTTERDON HILL, LOOKING N.

Approaching from Ivybridge, access to the open moor is through the field system, off the Harford Road above the main-line railway bridge, and is known as the beginning of the Two Moors Way. The first part of the path provides a gentle climb up to the saddle between Weatherdon and Butterdon Hills. Hangershell Rock is only half a mile distant and really much more of a feature than the sketch suggests.

Stalldon
Barrow.

Three Barrows.
Sharp
Tor.

Furon Down.

Erme Valley.

FROM TRISTIS ROCK. LOOKING N.

CROSSING page reference: 401 O.S.MAP reference: SX 638602
TITLE: FROM TRISTIS ROCK, LOOKING N.

This location is best approached up the Erme valley, following a path up the right bank. After a gate in the walled enclosure, cut up to the left. The two rock piles soon become visible, from which the view, as depicted in the sketch, is wonderful. Hugging the rounded bottom of the valley below Sharp Tor is Piles Copse, one of only three remaining ancient oak woods. Tristis Rock is sometimes known as Hall Tor.

Erme Valley.

ROM SOUTHERN SLOPE OF STALLDON BARROW.   LOOKING S.S.E.

CROSSING page reference: 402 O.S.MAP reference: SX 636614
TITLE: FROM SOUTHERN SLOPE OF STALLDON BARROW,
LOOKING S.E.
The point at which this sketch was drawn must have been determined
by the visibility of distant Ugborough Beacon over the near horizon,
and by the general alignment of Tristis Rock with Tor Rocks.
Obviously the River Erme was visible then, but it has since become
completely obscured by increased vegetation. Butterdon and
Weatherdon Hills are not as separate as the drawing suggests. Also,
two of the cairns on Weatherdon Hill are clearly visible on the
skyline.

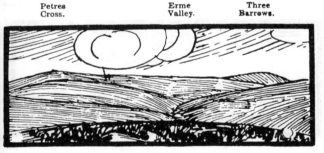

Petres   Erme   Three
Cross.   Valley.   Barrows.

FROM BROAD ROCK.   LOOKING S.E.

CROSSING page reference: 409 O.S.MAP reference: SX 618673
TITLE: FROM BROAD ROCK, LOOKING S.E.
Broad Rock is at a remote spot on the course of the Abbot's Way on
the southern slopes of Great Gnat's Head. The rock itself, inscribed
with its name and the boundary mark BB, does not really justify its
name. The area is best approached from Nun's Cross Farm (SX
605698). The bleak view down the Erme valley from Broad Rock
remains the same within the scope of the sketch. However, to the
left a new, man-made feature has emerged, that of Red Lake china
clay spoil tip.

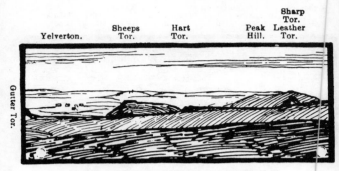

Yelverton. Sheeps Tor. Hart Tor. Peak Hill. Sharp Tor. Leather Tor.

Gutter Tor.

FROM NEAR BROAD ROCK. LOOKING N.W.

CROSSING page reference: 409 O.S.MAP reference: SX 617673
TITLE: FROM NEAR BROAD ROCK, LOOKING N.W.
The view from this position to the west of Broad Rock is panoramic
to the south and west, with views of Plymouth and the sea beyond,
and with the Cornish moors visible on a clear day, away to the
west. From this distance, it would never have been possible to make
out the individual buildings of Yelverton as the sketch might suggest,
and today the village is camouflaged by trees.

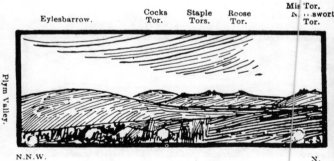

Eylesbarrow. Cocks Tor. Staple Tors. Roose Tor. Mis Tor. N. Hessworth Tor.

Plym Valley.

N.N.W.   N.

FROM NEAR BROAD ROCK.

CROSSING page reference: 410 O.S.MAP reference: SX 617673
TITLE: FROM NEAR BROAD ROCK
This sketch represents the view from a position to the west of Broad
Rock. Eylesbarrow is the most prominent feature, since it is just
the other side of the Plym valley and therefore much closer than the
other named features. From this position, North Hessary Tor, now
with its tall mast in evidence, is in direct line with Great Mis Tor
beyond. Roose Tor is now Roos Tor.

Shell Top.

Pen Beacon.

Clay Works.

FROM WHITEHALL, CORNER.   LOOKING E.

CROSSING page reference: 427 O.S.MAP reference: SX 5762
TITLE: FROM WHITEHALL CORNER, LOOKING E.
Whitehall Corner (now Whitehill) no longer exists as far as the
general public is concerned! The Cholwichtown Clay Works shown
in the sketch have since expanded almost beyond belief. By courtesy
of Mr. Brown, the area site manager, I was given a comprehensive
tour of the whole works, including what was once Whitehall Corner.
From this location a huge spoil tip completely obscures Pen Beacon
(now Penn), although Shell Top is still visible to the left.

Cooks Tor. Peak Hill. Sharp Tor. Lether Tor. Sheeps Tor. Mis Tor.   N. Hisworthy Tor.

Ringmoor

Trowlsworthy Warren.   Leggis Tor.

FROM BLACKATON CROSS.   LOOKING N.

CROSSING page reference: 428 O.S.MAP reference: SX 571630
TITLE: FROM BLACKATON CROSS, LOOKING N.
Cadover Bridge (SX 555646) is on the country road between Meavy
and Wotter. Immediately on the left is a metalled road which is
only shown as a track on the map, but which has been improved in
order to take ECC traffic. At the entrance to Lee Moor China Clay
works, the view behind has hardly changed at all. Trowlsworthy
Warren is rather more extensive now than depicted, and North
Hessary Tor now has its distinctive mast on top.

Leggis Tor.

Trowlsworthy Warren House. Hen Tor.

Plym. E.

FROM NEAR CADAFORD BRIDGE.

CROSSING page reference: 429 O.S.MAP reference: SX 556645
TITLE: FROM NEAR CADAFORD BRIDGE
Cadaford (now Cadover) Bridge allows the country road from
Meavy to Cornwood to cross the River Plym. Wherever you stand,
the river never looks quite like its depiction in the sketch. Maybe
the original standpoint has been obliterated since the whole
landscape to the south has radically changed as a result of china
clay workings. Whereas the distant horizon has not changed to the
north, the metalled track, overhead power lines and prefabricated
buildings close by are all recent developments.

Trowlsworthy Tors   Shell Top.   Pen Beacon.

Hen Tor.

E.   Plym.   S.E.

FROM CADAFORD BRIDGE.

CROSSING page reference: 430 O.S.MAP reference: SX 555646
TITLE: FROM CADAFORD BRIDGE
If you stand on the bridge to review this sketch, the River Plym will
seem more prominent than in the drawing. The building on the far
left under Hen Tor was once the warrener's house at Trowlsworthy
Warren. After years of neglect it has recently been revived and
extended as a pony-trekking centre. The rest of the distant view can
hardly have changed at all.

Cocks Tor.   White Tor. Pu Tor. Staple Tor.   Merivale Quarry.   Mis Tor.

N. Roborough Rock.   Vixen Tor.

FROM NEAR ROBOROUGH ROCK.

CROSSING page reference: 445 O.S.MAP reference: SX 515671
TITLE: FROM NEAR ROBOROUGH ROCK

The view from this location overlooking Roborough Rock has changed considerably since this sketch was drawn. The buildings on the outskirts of Yelverton are much the same, but the road was completely eradicated by the R.A.F. during the 2nd World War, although there is extensive vegetation visible now. In the sketch, some artistic licence has been used - Cocks Tor is in fact six miles away and Pu Tor (now Pew) is about four miles away.

Slope of Mis Tor.   Hollow Tor. Inga Tor.   N. Hisworthy Tor.   Dousland.   Peak Hill. Lether Tor.

King Tor.

FROM NEAR ROBOROUGH ROCK.

CROSSING page reference: 445 O.S.MAP reference: SX 515670
TITLE: FROM NEAR ROBOROUGH ROCK

The only way to experience this view is to proceed a little way up the hill along the country road which runs due south from Roborough Rock. The trees in the foreground are very extensive today and virtually obscure the main A386 Plymouth to Tavistock road. The village of Dousland has been developed considerably over the years, but remains at least partially hidden by trees. As with many of these sketches, the more distant features have been exaggerated to help identification - North Hisworthy Tor is in fact six miles away.

Lether Tor.   Down Tor.   Sheeps Tor.   Eylesbarrow.

Peak Hill.

Yennadon Down.   E.

FROM NEAR ROBOROUGH ROCK.

CROSSING page reference: 446 O.S.MAP reference: SX 515669
TITLE: FROM NEAR ROBOROUGH ROCK
If you walk up the minor road to the south of Roborough Rock, the
additional height achieved allows you to see over the trees to the
east. The field system shown in the sketch on the slopes of Yenneden
Down is now largely built-up, forming the outskirts of Dousland.
On the left, the trees of the Burrator Plantations are now visible
below Lether Tor. Down Tor only just appears over the horizon,
and is not as prominent as shown in the sketch.

S. Hisworthy
Hart Tor.   Tor.   Gramber Tor.

Sharp Tor.   Raddick Hill.   Lether Tor.

FROM SUMMIT OF PEAK HILL.   LOOKING N.E.

CROSSING page reference: 452 O.S.MAP reference: SX 556699
TITLE: FROM THE SUMMIT OF PEAK HILL, LOOKING N.E.
Hart Tor is rather insignificant below the horizon on the right of
Sharp Tor. On a clear day, the mast on top of North Hessary Tor can
be seen over the top of Sharpitor. The main difference in the scene
today is the encroachment of the conifer plantations, to the extent
that Raddick Farm, depicted on the slopes of Raddick Hill, has
long since been abandoned and lost to view.

Hen Gutter Shell Pen Trowlesworthy
Tor. Tor. Tor. Beacon. Tors.

Burrator Reservoir.

Sheeps Tor. Sheeps Tor
Village.

FROM THE SUMMIT OF PEAK HILL.

CROSSING page reference: 453 O.S.MAP reference: SX 556699
TITLE: FROM THE SUMMIT OF PEAK HILL
This sketch depicts the view facing south-east. We see Burrator
Reservoir as it was before the level was raised in 1928. The buildings
shown in the left foreground are probably Vinneylake Farm, now
abandoned and overwhelmed by the conifer plantations which now
virtually surround the reservoir. Today, there is one addition to the
far horizon. To the right of Trowlsworthy Tors, the flat-topped spoil
tips of Lee Moor china clay works are clearly visible.

Brent Barn Cox Staple Roose White Great Links Mis
Tor. Hill. Tor. Tors. Tor. Tor. Tor Tor.
                                          Hare Tor

Pu Tor

Quarry.

Vixen Tor. Inga Tor. King Tor.
FROM POND ON PEAK HILL. LOOKING N.

CROSSING page reference: 453 O.S.MAP reference: SX 557706
TITLE: FROM POND ON PEAK HILL, LOOKING N.
The quarry on the right is Swelltor Quarry. Below it, contouring
around King Tor, the trackbed of the Princetown branch railway
line from Yelverton can be seen. This was closed under the so-
called 'Beeching axe' in 1956, but it has recently been revived as a
cycle track. Brent Tor is in fact well off the moor beyond Tavistock,
but from this location appears to be part of it.

Foggin Tor Hollow Quarry. Tor. N Hisworthy Tor. Leedon Tor. Princetown Church.

N.E.

FROM POND ON PEAK HILL.

CROSSING page reference: 454 O. S .MAP reference: SX 557706
TITLE: FROM POND ON PEAK HILL
The pond in question is just to the right of the B3212 road as it
levels off after its climb up on to the moor from Yelverton. The
modern road is only slightly more obtrusive as it falls out of sight
towards Princetown whose church tower can still just be seen,
despite the fact that a copse of evergreen trees is gradually obscuring
this feature.

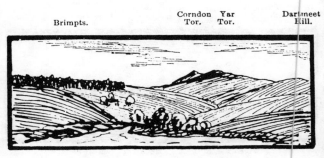

Brimpts. Corndon Tor. Yar Tor. Dartmeet Hill.

FROM FOREST INN, HEXWORTHY.

CROSSING page reference: 457 O. S .MAP reference: SX 654726
TITLE: FROM FOREST INN, HEXWORTHY
The Forest Inn, which must have been immediately behind F.G.S.
when he drew this sketch, re-opened for business in August 1992,
following several months of closure. Corndon Tor is obscured by
Yar Tor from this position and so it must be Corndon Down that is
visible immediately to the left. Today, the mature trees in the
foreground partly obscure the middle distance, but not enough to
see that the layout of hills and valleys is actually rather different
from that depicted in the sketch!

Sharp Tor.   Holne Moor.   Bench Tor.   Paignton Reservoir.

FROM THE ROAD AT TOP OF DARTMEET HILL. LOOKING DUE S.

CROSSING page reference: 460 O.S.MAP reference: SX 682734
TITLE: FROM THE ROAD AT THE TOP OF DARTMEET HILL, LOOKING DUE S.

Sharp Tor, Bench Tor and the slopes of Yartor Down on the right appear to be about right, although the view is more to the south-east than due south. Holne Moor is the high ground beyond Paignton Reservoir (now obscured from view by the encircling band of trees). The sketch also suggests some obvious enclosures on the near slopes of Bench Tor, no evidence of which exists today!

Combestone Tor   Holne Ridge.   Down Ridge.

S.E.   Huccaby.   S.

FROM THE ROAD NEAR HUCCABY COTTAGE.

CROSSING page reference: 461 O.S.MAP reference: SX 661735
TITLE: FROM THE ROAD NEAR HUCCABY COTTAGE

Huccaby Cottage, now somewhat modernised, is the last house on the right after climbing up the hill from Dartmeet on the main B3357 road towards Two Bridges. There is considerably more vegetation now on this side of the Dart valley, so that Huccaby Farm in the centre foreground looks less like an oasis, and Huccaby House, further down, is now almost totally obscured. In this sketch, there is no sign of the country road that runs down past the farm to Hexworthy bridge.

Bellaford Tor.

Lough Tor.

Dunnabridge Pound.

FROM SWINCOMBE NEWTAKE. LOOKING N. BY E.

CROSSING page reference: 463 O.S.MAP reference: SX 637728
TITLE: FROM SWINCOMBE NEWTAKE, LOOKING N. BY E.
Approaching the Swincombe Valley from the country road above
the Forest Inn at Hexworthy, extensive ancient walled enclosures,
or 'newtakes' appear on both sides of the valley. If you walk along
the SWWA access road up the valley as far as the Fairy Bridge
footbridge, the remains of Swincombe Farm and surrounding
newtakes are just on the right. Follow the grassy path leaving the
farm, for a little way and the features in the sketch will come into
line. Today, the tree line of the Bellever Plantations can be seen on
the horizon.

White Ridge.

Water Hill.
Meripit Hill.

Birch Tor.

Post Bridge.

FROM LAKEHEAD HILL. LOOKING N.E.

CROSSING page reference: 469 O.S.MAP reference: SX 6478
TITLE: FROM LAKEHEAD HILL, LOOKING N.E.
Apart from a wide grassy strip over the top of the hill, beginning at
Kraps Ring Settlement, this whole area has become part of the
Bellever Forestry Plantations. Both Assycombe Hill (which P.G.S.
left out of his sketch!) and White Ridge are now on the perimeter
of the Fernworthy Plantations and the two areas of tree-lined horizon
have changed the scene quite significantly anyway.The houses on
the left of the road are now surrounded by mature trees.

Bellaford Tor.   Lakehead Hill.   Bairdown Tor.   Longaford Tor.

Pizwell.

FROM SOUSSONS COMMON. LOOKING W.

CROSSING page reference: 472 O.S.MAP reference: SX 6779
TITLE: FROM SOUSSONS COMMON, LOOKING W.
Soussons Common (now Soussons Down) is now a Forestry
Plantation and so it would be futile to try and find the exact location
from which this sketch was drawn. However, the area to the west
of the country road at Ephraim's Pinch allows a reasonable
alternative. The extensive plantations around Bellever have also
transformed the view. Bellever Tor is two miles distant, whereas
Beardown and Longaford Tors are four miles away.

Birch Tor.   Challacombe Down.   Hameldon.

FROM SOUSSONS COMMON. LOOKING N.E.

CROSSING page reference: 473 O.S.MAP reference: SX 6779
TITLE: FROM SOUSSONS COMMON, LOOKING N.E.
Since all of Soussons Common is covered with conifers, the view
depicted by this sketch no longer exists. The three distant features
are virtually unchanged and can be seen from a point to the south-
east of Ephrain's Pinch (SX 679784) where there is rising open
grassland. The country road, which follows the perimeter of the
plantation down the hill to Runnage Bridge, meets the main B3212
road above Postbridge at the bottom of Merripit Hill.

Bellaford Tor.   S. Hisworthy Tor.   Princetown Church.   N. Hisworthy Tor.

FROM MERIPIT HILL. LOOKING S.W.

CROSSING page reference: 474 O.S.MAP reference: SX 662801
TITLE: FROM MERIPIT HILL, LOOKING S.W.
Meripit is now Merripit. Princetown Church is actually six miles away and deliberately enlarged for the purpose of identification. The village of Postbridge is obscured by the trees in the foreground and the road to Princetown beyond is now the B3212. The whole of the central area from Bellever to this road below Lakehead Hill is now covered by conifer plantation, thus transforming this view.

Littaford Tor.   Longaford Tor.   Higher White Tor.

Powder Mills.

FROM ROAD AT LAKEHEAD HILL. LOOKING W. TO N.W.

CROSSING page reference: 478 O.S.MAP reference: SX 634771
TITLE: FROM ROAD AT LAKEHEAD HILL, LOOKING W. TO N.W.
Powder Mills was the necessarily remote location chosen for the dangerous production of gunpowder during the 19th century, supplying the mining and quarrying industries. One of the two remaining chimneys is depicted - the other (and the main row of houses, now a craft centre) - is situated further to the left. The building on the right is now in a rather more ruinous state. The dotted lines in the sketch below Longaford Tor are dry-stone walled enclosures or newtakes.

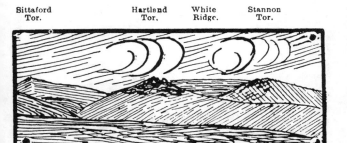

Sittaford Tor.   Hartland Tor.   White Ridge.   Stannon Tor.

FROM NEAR ARCHERTON. LOOKING N.N.E.

CROSSING page reference: 479 O.S.MAP reference: SX 641794
TITLE: FROM NEAR ARCHERTON, LOOKING N.N.E.
Starting from Postbridge, Drift Lane is the well-marked path
between the East Dart on the right and the enclosures of Archerton
on the left. The view from the hill looking back over the Dart valley
corresponds exactly with the sketch. New to the horizon are the
tops of the conifer trees on White Ridge and on Assycombe Hill to
the right of Stannon Tor. These are on the perimeter of the
Fernworthy Plantations.

Black Ridge.   Ockment Hill.   Cranmere X   Hangingstone Steeperton. Hill.

White Horse Hill

FROM CUT HILL. LOOKING N.

CROSSING page reference: 479 O.S.MAP reference: SX 598827
TITLE: FROM CUT HILL, LOOKING N.
Now that Cranmere is relatively accessible from the military road,
Cut Hill which is the third highest point, must arguably be the most
remote feature on the northern moor. Hangingstone Hill is the same
height and it is interesting that, in this sketch, this name is used,
rather than its old name, Newtake, which was used in two of the
other sketches (pages 485 and 486).

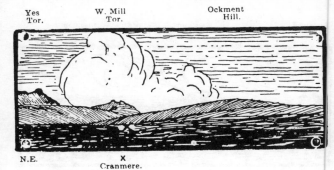

Yes Tor. W. Mill Tor. Ockment Hill.

N.E. X
Cranmere.

FROM ¼ MILE WEST OF E. DART HEAD.

CROSSING page reference: 480 O.S.MAP reference: SX 603854
TITLE: FROM 1/4 M. WEST OF E. DART HEAD
If you are approaching Cranmere Pool from the south, the view to the north is spectacular. Cranmere itself was first mentioned as Crawmere-pool in *Polwhele's Historical Views of Devon* in 1793. A few years later, in 1802, Mr. E.A. Bray (later vicar of Tavistock) noted that the so-called pool was in fact dry! It is supposedly haunted by a former Mayor of Okehampton who appears as a black colt or as an ugly dwarf known as Binjie Gear.

Great Kneeset. Black Ridge. Cranmere X

CROSSING page reference: 481 O.S.MAP reference: SX 586843
TITLE: FROM LITTLE KNEESET, LOOKING N.E.
Bearing the shape of Great Kneeset in mind, the more westerly, but lower part of this ridge to the south is clearly Little Kneeset. If you are making for Cranmere Pool (a point beyond the horizon in this sketch), then the best route from Fur Tor is through the Peat Pass over the higher part of this ridge, and the longer pass over the summit of Black Ridge. These are known as the Phillpotts Passes and are marked at either end with a standing stone each bearing a metal plate inscribed as follows:-THIS STONE MARKS A CROSSING THROUGH THE PEAT, WHICH MAY BE OF USE TO HUNTING AND CATTLEMEN; THE CROSSING WAS MADE BY FRANK PHILLPOTTS WHO DIED OCTOBER 1909. IT IS KEPT UP IN HIS MEMORY BY HIS BROTHER AND SON.

Cut Hill.   Black Ridge.

X
Cranmere.

FROM SOUTHERN SLOPE OF OCKMENT HILL, ABOUT ¼ M. S.E. OF SUMMIT.

CROSSING page reference: 482 O.S.MAP reference: SX 604874
TITLE: FROM SOUTHERN SLOPE OF OKEMENT HILL,
ABOUT 1/4 M. S. E. OF SUMMIT
These days, approaching Cranmere Pool from the north is the easiest
way because it is possible to reach the top of Okement Hill by car,
using the road from the moor gate (now a cattle grid) by the military
camp above Okehampton. Okement Hill is easily recognisable by
the army lookout bunker on top. This location is just over a mile
from Cranmere Pool 'as the crow flies', but rather more if travelling
through the Peat Pass and following the West Okement river.

Great   Great Links   Amicombe
Kneeset.   Tor.   Hill.

X
Cranmere.

FROM NEAR SUMMIT OF NEWTAKE.

CROSSING page reference: 485 O.S.MAP reference: SX 616861
TITLE: FROM NEAR SUMMIT OF NEWTAKE
Cranmere Pool became distinctive in 1854 when James Perrott of
Chagford built a cairn there and placed in it a bottle for the receipt
of visitors' cards, thereby establishing the first 'letter-box' on the
moor. By the 1950s there were other 'letter-boxes' on the southern
moor. They were so-called because it had become traditional to
stamp a self-addressed postcard, leave it in the box, and remove
and post any cards left there by the previous visitors.

Black Ridge.   Great Kneeset.   Great Links Tor.   Amicombe Hill

W.   **x**
Cranmere.

FROM NEWTAKE,. ⅓ M. S. OF SUMMIT

CROSSING page reference: 486 O.S.MAP reference: SX 616855
TITLE: FROM NEWTAKE 1/3 M. S. OF SUMMIT

This sketch would be useful if you were approaching Cranmere Pool from the west, say from Scorhill Down. Newtake in this case was Newtake Hill, now always known as Hangingstone Hill, and distinctive these days for the army observation post on top. There was no accurate count of the number of walkers who found Cranmere Pool until two Plymouth-based ramblers, Mr. H. P. Hearder and Mr. H. Scott Tucker, placed a visitors' book there in 1905. By December 1908, 1,741 signatures had been recorded that year alone.

Great Links Tor.   Amicombe Hill.   Foresland Ledge.

x
Cranmere.   FROM NEAR E. DART HEAD.   N.W.

CROSSING page reference: 488 O.S.MAP reference: SX 608855
TITLE: FROM NEAR E. DART HEAD

This location is not a particularly pleasant one for the walker because of the ground underfoot - basically peat bog with islands of turf! However, there is little alternative if Cranmere Pool is your objective and you are approaching from the direction of Fernworthy or Postbridge in the south-west. Foresland Ledge is now Fordsland Ledge. The spectacular valley between this and Amicombe Hill is the dramatic route that the West Okement river takes off the north-western edge of the high moor.